Bardo:
Parable of Tomorrow

Ishmael Fiifi Ayerebi Annobil is a Ghanaian poet, journalist, multi-award winning filmmaker, photographer, artist, emblemist, and digital composer. He was born in 1958, in Accra, Ghana, where he started writing poetry at the age of eleven, and entered journalism soon after high school. He has lived in the Sudan and Kenya, where he perfromed his acclaimed recital for the homeless and landless, (Nairobi 1983), and worked as a reporter, before moving to England as a correspondent, in the same year. In 1987, he moved with his family to Wales, where he founded the international poetry festival, *Iolo's Children (*now *Festival Iolo*), and Wales' first serious arts newspaper, *Circa21*. He is the founder/editor of online arts journal *Chiaroscuro Magazine*, and the London film collective, *Stonedog Productions* (London). His films include, *Linda Karshan: Covid-19 Conversation*, a multi-award winning documentary about American minimalist artist Linda Karshan; *In The Presence of Awe - The Transvangarde* (art documentary), *Kenji Yoshida - Artist of the Soul* (art documentary), *Salamander Walks* (a surreal feature), *Hornsleth: Product of Love* (documentary), and currently finishing the definitive documentary about Karshan, *Choreographing the Page*. In 2023 he and his cinematographer daughter, Nana Yaa, co-directed *Insomnia*, an innovative, multi-award winning film based on his eponymous monograph. He has published two other volumes of poetry, *Seven Horn Elegy* and *Ethiop*, and one music album, *Zingliwu*. His forthcoming books include *Portrait of a Man in Pain* (novel), and *Inklings of Clay* (historical novella). He is the creator of *Abëtëi*, a body of philosophical emblems for the Gadangme people of Ghana, which he views as his greatest achievement. A master photographer, his images have been published in various publications, including *The Independent Newspaper*, and prestigious French magazine *M3*. Ishmael attended Christian Methodist Secondary School (Accra, Ghana), studied Social Anthropology extramurally at Goldsmith's College, and undertook a PgDip in Visual Communications at West Herts College. He now lives in Ghana.

Bardo:
Parable of Tomorrow
(poems for my mother)

ISHMAEL FIIFI ANNOBIL

Published in England by Totem, in 2024
Totem, 60 Swinley House, Redhill Street, London NW1 4BB, UK

© Ishmael Fiifi Ayerebi Annobil

All rights reserved under all international copyright laws and conventions.

ISBN: 978-1-899151-15-8

Designed and typeset by Ishmael Fiifi Annobil

Cover illustration: Senufo hornbill (*Sejen*) from Côte D'Ivoire, symbolising the male and female components of life; Copyright © The Africarium Collection, Paris.

Author's Portrait: by Nana Yaa Annobil © 2018; at Abbazia di San Giorgio Maggiore

*So God created mankind in his own image,
in the image of God he created them;
male and female he created them.*
— Genesis 1:27

Table of Contents

9	Of Horses and Airs
10	She Came To Me That Night
11	The Appearance of Colour
12	Ao!
13	Tones of Myrrh
14	The Christian Invisibility Thing
15	Naming History
16	A Vesuvian Coitus
17	Domestication
18	Where Doves Die
19	Depression
20	Cenote
21	Nocturne
22	Rain Watchers
23	The Procession
24	The Oud Player
25	It Tiptoes
26	The Enemy
27	Africa Um-Ah
28	The Dead Forest by the Nile
29	An American Crucifixion
30	Fire
31	A Rainbow Blooms in the North
32	Roma
34	Water
35	To Tame a Horse
36	We the People
37	Promise of Feathers
38	This Chief of Staff
39	24th February 1966
40	These Scientists!
41	Lineage
42	A Great Sun Retires
43	Parable of Tomorrow
44	Ladies and Others
45	Quietude
46	Bird Without Song
47	We May Never Know

To the memory of my beloved mother
Hannah Aku Annobil (née Gberbie)

To Mama

Of Horses and Airs

Whenever you climb onto a horse's back,
Remember he or she is your mother (yes, her),
For the duration of your vanity, when
Your hubris impinges on its bigger soul.

Remember, yes, remember the risks it takes
To manage the giddy stack on its back,
Against whom rebellion only gains nudged
And whipped pain, or nuanced chemistry.

Make sure to feel it's hacking throat in yours,
Its hacking heart bracing against disgracing peril,
As you test your mettle against thorned scrub
And the sparked silence of stingrayed rivers.

Hear your mother's rasping breath couched in
Its neigh, like the knot of a cyst, like broken love,
When you play Pegasus into the roosting sun,
Bathed in silhouettes of vampire bats.

(7 November, 2017, 1:32 am, Regents Park, London)

For my ancestral mothers

She Came To Me That Night

Something pure and unsaid made me
Turn away from my wailing soul,
Fix my footing in the shifting sand,
And forget, like a broken mirror, the asps,
Assassins, and their bog-wet progeny
Besetting me, as foretold by the oracle;
Hissing and jostling like eels to take my heart
Into the sewers with them.

And there she was, folded out of time,
The fabled queen of Bahia, glass-beautiful
Spirit of the Middle Passage (Obsidian),
Tingling the mooned-night with her
Swirling velvet skirt of bells; silver conchs
Tuned to a cosmic key, asymmetric like
The mirth of love and providence – jazz.
Only I could see her, this vivacious deity!

She sailed through the heaving throngs,
Unseen and untouched, haloed by
Golden light like the Black Madonna,
Smiling shyly without looking at me, and
I felt all of her in me—mine only to hold;
She was here to heal me, her descendant,
On this brimstoned path of our Diaspora,
Because my pain had transcended me.

(12 July 2020, 11:16pm, London)

For Jill Silverman Van Coenegrachts

The Appearance of Colour

It rose like an amen from the baft[1]
Unstained with milk curd or the elemental
Aura of seed and postnatallia

It rose, that's some word, it rose
Vertically through a visiting mist, marking
The path to freedom and quest—an amen

Rimmed in Bedouin, even Tuareg blue-black
Blazed in two by an orange flame
Trembling like the vibrato of a whisper.

And I ran into myself to listen
To stop that pinging clamour of my breath
From drowning this new lovely love of mine

Let's call it colour, a good word,
It does not restrain or shackle humility—stain it!
It adulterates it with the benign arsenic of rebellion.

So here I am.
All of me.
Not a wept thing.

(14 November 2019, 5.15pm, Regents Park, London)

---

1. Baft: a coarse fabric, usually cotton or linen, or plain woven material

Ao!

If the milk churn were brutalism itself,
There would be a settling of doubts; I mean,
Into simple truths for *their*[1] simple selves to thank.

Passé, they call me; bathos, if I am lucky
Because the churn is still a churn, yoke of yokes,
Nowhere near brutalist, not by any measure – hey.

So I remain the sonorous, scintillating cipher
Preyed in the dark by sin and lust without earshot of
The chisel-tap of a decipherer (tainted anthropology)

      Every morning, life rises to burn itself again
      And the altar it burns upon plays a grateful
      Homily like the grunting and bells of yaks – bells.

Listen to me, there is a sweet river beneath all that—
Helloo!? I hear it above all the morass and um and ah
Of these great leaders of humankind – bunch of lotharios.

There's your answer then;
The milk churn can hear things like binaural clear, with
Space between for thinking hearts and minds to dance.

Ao-ao, laugh some, if you dare kill this pain.

(14 November 2019, 6.15pm, Regents Park, London)

---

1. Men.

Tones of Myrrh

At the dawn of the pulsating knot
– Things that are prurient-impure –
When a man's voice buckles your knees

When the fire of your sacred hearth
Blazes at your unschooled touch, and
Sweet tones of myrrh lead you in and out

Of the delirium of love and shame—
The monastic fugue, when you are at your most
Pure, and so prone to the baffling pain of loss;

When the earth you walk on
Becomes a sleigh of woes, tempered by those
Secret triumphs you daren't mention by name

For they are sin. But are they?

(14 November 2019, 6.15pm, Regents Park, London)

The Christian Invisibility Thing

Fate brings us here, not logic or God
— God creates; fate is a determiner, determined
By a sleight of hand too far back for the human eye.

Take yourself for instance;
You have it in your bones and muscles to undo the heck
But the thought alone kills you, makes you feel a sham.

Letting others open the jar for you
Is one of the ways you enthrone fools,
Lest animus, totally unhinged animus, get in your face.

(14 November 2019, 20:23pm, Regents Park, London)

Naming History

Write your name in this mud,
It's flowing too fast not to.
Let your name sink into its waves
Like the discarded potato that raises a nation.
Haven't you not heard of the garrotted man
In the bog with his leather pouch of dreams?
Or his female counterpart, who they'd
Un-souled like a sacral lamb?
These were written into the mud by men,
I say, by men infatuated with tar and feather,
Drawings, quarterings—sick men.
Yet they transcend the bog like gods
Of a cloud mountain—Thunderbirds of pain.

You must write your name yourself.
Pray and blow onto it and watch it sink
Like a spent canoe. Let it sink so far down
As to feign obeisance — it's your treasure.
Let no one write it's obituary for you,
Or it'll hide from your memory,
And swear yourself to secrecy;
You owe nothing to no one.
Let it lie down there quietly;
It will petrify into black sequoia
In the uterine chemistry—rare breed.
Worry not, it will rise to the surface
When the blinkers finally give way, demystified
Like gored matadors in blazing sunshine.

(16 November, 2019; 12:42am, Regents Park, London)

A Vesuvian Coitus

Charred coitus, caught in the jaws of fury,
Eyeless sockets still sharing empathy,
Your auras waxing turquoise against the
Charcoal of your last deed. You are here
Compromised for posterity to mourn or mock;

Nearly solemn as though your coitus were
A sacrament—fertility rite or assuaging swansong.
There may have been something more between
Your soulless coils, we hope, though you howl
At each other like fish against hearth.

Were you drunk, you snarling souls, were you drunk,
Or were you sallow from your drained veins;
Did you enjoy the small death before your deaths,
Or even feel the frenzied clawing at each other's back;
Was there a coincidence between heaven and hell
As your eyes rolled back with the rapture and pain
—what flashed on your retinas before the curtain fall?

Did you imagine the Madonna interceding,
Even as you hastened your rapture; did you fall
In love just before dying; did you weep or wail;
Did you try to kiss against the spring of desiccation;
Did you imagine an afterlife, or were you mere
Fatalists with a simple gold coin between you;

Was it the Stabat Mater or the laughter of Hercules
You heard at the peak of your evacuation,
Or did you just see a tussle between gods?
Are you looking down on me now with white wings,
Or looking up mournfully at me with fiery wings?

I mourn you.

(22 April 2009, Regents Park, London)

Domestication

The air we breathe is full of sibilants
We animate, fret and feather it like that
To domesticate ourselves (Adam and Eve) or
We'd be grunting humanoids, like hoe-heads
Without handles, whetstone, or heath to tame.

What of nymphs or the prophetic cicadas?
Is their own air self-shorn or unshorn?
What dreams spring from their articulacy?
Do they also 'mare ghouls and phantoms
Like we do when our minds take in ether?

What of the free-flowing river (fey honey);
It's slurping sonnets and hooting mantras,
Honouring always with its cooling fire?
Is it her sibilant rivulets or warbling twerks
That draw us, or are we deeply amphibian?

(29 November 2019, 8:30pm, Regents Park, London)

Where Doves Die

Life nowadays requires a victim at
Every turn: solemnity died; sanctimony
Reigns like the an eternal monarch.

Politics is the unearthly ability to darken
Nature; organise mass human sacrifice,
To sate the almighty trash-gods of id.

Celebrity is broken dolls with fish lips,
Enacted by a scalpel and invisible spider's
Web; bedraggled fashion; and toxic egos.

Love itself walks the plank, unkempt, open-
Mouthed like a basking shark, teasing,
Waiting for small things, then dies.

(29 May 2009, 2.50am, Regents Park)

Depression

Mind weevil—cold page of a silenced book
Preyed upon by stale memory and sick contrition,
Self-doubt, chiefly, and the scent of death.

Smirched with thin clay, as if grazed
By a passing leviathan; a lost pterodactyl with
An eye only for the past – a big nothing.

Airless rambles, always airless, through
Dark heaths, muddy meadows, and siren-vales
That wail like clarions of a foretold debacle.

Stand up! aim for your soul's pirouetting light,
Let it through your dark veil— let it hypnotise you,
And take you to the fire dance.

(18 May 2017, 1:40, Regents Park, London)

Cenote

Water's own apotheosis, sweetened with imagining:
Domain of spirits and human nematodes —
Ghosts of sacrificial lambs, hissing and cackling,
Not seen but heard in deep thinking ears.

This light-danced realm, pure and foreboding like
An imminent deflowering on the cusp of want.
Dreams are trapped in such heart-in-mouth element —
Off dreams of hopers and wanton nihilists alike.

This sacral water has tasted all sorts of blood and gore
(Would you believe?), humans churned out of life
Like prairie rats, to keep a smile on the face of the sun.
We can't stand here any longer than our faiths can bear.

(12 October 2017, 8:20, Regents Park, London)

Nocturne

I am observing this haunted night from my balcony.
The two great totems of the otherworld have
Lost the love and hate between them, for now:
The brass gong has tolled its last, the blessed
Motets of yore are not turning hearts, and the muezzin's
Megaphone is shorn of air—there is a loss.

Beyond the spire and minaret, a silver-black sea
Shimmers like Mesmer's cape, heaving tankers and whales
On its broad shoulders (straining anchor and slumber).
There will be no rainstorm tonight, that much I know;
There is no wind to stir the clouds to such grand mirth.
The biosphere is asleep.

There is no lightning to jump-start things, no bats, no owl,
The dogs are not howling, not the faintest anguish of colic
On a night like this, or the song of a retreating motorbike
—Just the weight of a coming, a frightful coming.
I am all alone, covered in spiders, but I won't leave this night;
It is mine, I bought it with my love, I will not desert it.

(27 May 2018, 11:12pm, Regents Park, London)

Rain Watchers

The wind tunnel between our blocks skeins and hisses
With mellow rain—jazz notes on a summer morn.
You are on your large state-owned balcony, smoking,
I am in my small private window like a vole, with opera;
All the birds are under your eaves like cherubs,
I have none to pamper, I have no eaves — crows
Scratch and poop at my window to get at my iron hen.

You emerge slowly through the combed water
Like an iconic bantamweight, hooded, Italian maybe,
Wafer-thin and aquiline with the enigma of a boxer,
Pulling on your thin, long joint at an angle—tomboy
(Exemplar of the waywardness age has stolen from me);
We own this rain alone, like opposite border guards
Cutting each other some slack—can't whip life.

       Callas[1] paints *Orfeo and Eurydice* into the chasm!

We are a very exclusive club, you and me;
We are beyond the warbling right-wing zeitgeist,
The looming divorce[2] conjured by a drunken pixie.
We must hold on to this moment, my funky sister:
Divorce or not, nature will always rain on its earth.
Let this fact comfort you, as you become a foreigner,
And I remain the foreigner I have always loved being.

(3 November, 2018, London)

1: Maria Callas, Greek opera singer, 1923-1977 (this line refers to a background radio broadcast); 2: Brexit

The Procession

Such is our proud avatar for the Second Coming:
He fronts the ecstatic vigil, facing east,
This priest, no, Monsignor, caped with our woes,
Arrogantly pious with a creased forehead
Like God's only bearer of the mendicant's bushel.
"I am the one given onto you for succour," he says.
But he abhors the cap of martyrdom and the humble
Crust, though he leans that way in speech.
Like all else on God's earth, he animates only
When faith deigns to prostate like wax before him,
All-burred and thrustful like dawn's first piss.
But we need his rarefied facility, O, he knows that,
So, he usurps the Cross, poised to cast the first stone
When the Messiah returns, for he is the antichrist.

(17 December, 2019, 23:43, London)

The Oud Player

In all my dreams I play the oud to all the tribes of God,
From Aden to the charred hillsides of Kurdistan
Even the oil choked gorges and plains of Azerbaijan;
In spite of the sweet-scented water that carries death
Like a love potion to the possessed dervish on his
Cusp of eternity; his tongue folded in two by pain.

In all my dreams I play the oud, O this carrier of love,
I play my oud to God's lovelorn tribes below the Sahel,
From Timbuktu to the parched *zongos* of the dejected;
To the howling palaces where ants scream and die for water,
And to the vultures in vigil over the bony ghosts of cows
Torn between a forsaken heaven and weightless grass.

In all my dreams I play my oud at red-eyed monsters
From Soweto to the plastic acres of the Gulf of Guinea,
Even at the dazzling prophets trapped in stupefied harems,
With winged serpents coiled around golden obelisks
Like sentinels of a sacred oases, where lepers become gods;
Till the scarlet dawn, when my oud banishes them to hades.

(4 March, 2020, 2:23am, London)

It Tiptoes

Nature tiptoes around us like
A golden crested fowl elected
By lore to crouch at a shrine
And be cut and bled for its glory.
        It tiptoes in case our hunger is
A mere figment that can be lured
And betrayed by self-love then
Taught to tread like a bushfire
Seeking its reflection in a lake.

(16 May 2020, 02:40 am, London)

The Enemy

        I don't choose my enemies.

They pick me out of the hordes
Because I smile like the sun.
They are wired to a dead moon
Far away in a churlish cosmos
Where hollow souls scavenge
And rape each other for venom.

To tell the truth, the most odious ones
Stole a ride in mother's sacred womb
As amniotic lice, jigger and djinn;
They are that intergalactic, these witches.
        I don't choose my enemies,
           I am a poet.

(11 June 2020, London)

Africa Um-Ah

It takes a hot fire
To make fat melt and spread,
To sear a thick crust under rice,
To pass from large mouth to little mouth.

(18 June 2020, 1:25pm, Regents Park)

The Dead Forest by the Nile

I cried yesterday into the sun
Like a stray dog, pure with hunger.

I prayed yesterday into the rocks
Like a shaken lizard, wan with revenge.

> I surmised from your smile that
> Forests can forsake huntsmen.

I reached yesterday into your pockets
Like a hapless urchin, wet with innocence.

I pored yesterday into your eyes
Like a battered orphan, drunk with pain.

> I surmised from your grimace that
> Houses can forsake builders.

I rummaged yesterday into the night
Like a stolen child, heavy with longing.

I raced yesterday into the dust storm
Like a sorcerer, armed with ploughs.

> I surmised from your chuckle that
> Africa, too, can forsake Africans.

(10 December, 2005, 12-48am, London)

To the memory of George Floyd

An American Crucifixion

Hallelujah!

A man has surpassed himself in death —
Drawn the hordes out of their bondages,
To breach the siege of bathos and gore.
Each awakened soul is God's masterpiece
For the rutting season of martyrs and bards.
Their song is free of cloud-dark augury, orbs,
And the cat fingers of dead-inside sorcerers.

Amen!

(20 June 2020, 18:06, Regents Park)

Fire

What is the way of the poet?

      Is it the quiet insanity
That sings like fish
In hot water?

Where on earth do you raise
These muses that defy space
Like spiders,
And yet strike metal pristine
Without a roaring furnace?

What is your way, or are you
      Just the messenger?

I say to you,
      When pushing yourself,
      Please listen to the feet you crush –
or you'll fail this quest;

When asleep,
      Let your soul wander
      To the old hill
      Where ancestors rest and
      Wait in judgement – appease them;

When rich with pain,
      Turn around once in a while
      To shed a tear for
      Those you left behind.

(17/7/2001, Islington.)

A Rainbow Blooms in the North

The friendly Irish lady who glad-ragged to attend
Leroy Francis' funeral, though she was new here,
Attempts to lift her granddaughter with her neck
To touch hands with an eager cat up a balcony.

She fails without recoiling, grappling on with
Hope firmly in her hands, till she spots me, and
Draws me in with *that* slanted Irish entreaty:
"Maybe this tall gentleman will let you sit on his
Shoulders to reach it—he's much taller than I."

Alas, I cannot sniff a cat without chancing asphyxia,
Nor can the whole six-foot-one of me bridge the
Electricity between the would-be lovers, even as
The cat cocks its head and drops its paw to us.

Just then a rainbow blooms to the north of us —
"We are meant to see this," says the friendly lady,
Tapping my arm the way older sisters do. It sinks.
How she glows, this beautiful Irish soul, who sang
So movingly at Leroy Francis' funeral.

(2 August 2020, 4:29pm, London)

Roma

This suspicion you encounter is inborn; as if
They blame you for the Moon's loss of hair
(you and your arcane arts that decipher the stars and fate);
As if you stole her tresses to trade for gold
On this earth that stays surprised by your eyes: as if
You were a wounded serpent seeking pity from piety

But you'd landed well, Roma, with the whirlwind

They say you came feet first into the clayey aftermath,
Recalcitrant like a feathered egg, mysterious,
An instant crowd disperser, though you smiled,
Fitful in your garnerer's quest for innermost things;
Seeking not, however, a mirror to judge your back –
This was the first impression, and also the last

The innocence you defeated would ache

You stood out amongst the elemental glories,
Including men; all so pristine, while they all
Jostled and pulsed for the tail-end of the fever
That breathed in their chests and stamens,
And you, unwise sage, stepped out and offered it –
No, brandished it with glee like a horny mustang

The beneficiaries took it away then spat at you

Thus marked, you retreated quietly, first lesson learnt,
To the borders of time, foraging for the truth
You'd handed over, making forays in and out of
The growing antipathy of man, teasing, as always,
With a gleaming groin when magic failed, till your self-betrayal
became your yoke, then the earth opened up under your feet.

So they say; but I say different – I am a poet, I write through fire.

I say, envy has many faces – but mostly oblique like
The hindquarters of a deflowered dog. They fear you;
You with your fired eyes that unravel hearts –
The very eyes their mothers creep to, at night, to decant their
Self-doubt and self-hate, to dissect the oracle on
Matters procreative, and of atrophied love – astral greed.

The spouses and progeny of those sleepwalkers envy you

For you ride on the shoulders of Chaos. Abandon is the
Panacea for your afflictions, and you don't cry like them –
So they think. Hence proud palisades greet your mysterious
Smile (lest you raise an ache in their groin; you with your
Allure, navy-blue like a chip off the old sky), though
Their children smile at you through the palisades.

The lingo you coined out of the morass still adorns nature

Till the tendrils of your journey fall off your soles,
The lordships' horses will crave your gentle breath—your
Echo will ring in their proud hearts like the afterbirth of a
Harp's strum, giddy and fantastical in the rhythm of blood
 – did you not invent the language of horses? Did you
Not burnish yew and pull sinew for fire-music?

Yet volcanoes raise more pathos than your tears

You've often warned them of the tarantula, the limbsome
Figure of apathy that engulfs us, but they shun the rituals:
The ecstatic trances and sacral cloths and waters
That you press to the earth's breast to neuter the absinthian
Smugness. You tell them you are no deluded Ofeo,
But they yawn like pussycats. Tally-hoo, they say to you.

O, soulful mendicant with a retreating ego

Your very knowledge has cast doubt on your sanity;
So they wail, Yesu Christo, Christ Almighty! whenever your
Shadow falls across their faces as if it were a languid devil's –
Ironic, you may say, because you, too, fell out of the vessel at
Joppa, Sanctified for the Christian harvest; blue-black though
for all the Elbows and shoulders bracing the opening.

You are still waiting to be touched

Turn around, Roma, turn away from the numbing wall,
And that hollow nerves called humanity, which batters
Your every step like thorns of the narrow path.
Tear them down with your mystique, as you would the
Medusas of your many crossroads, then turn around—
God wants to see your face, too.

(17/8/2003, Bloomsbury, London, 5pm)

Water

Every drop of water
Contains a grain of God

—Atheist know this better
Than the rest of us

It balms the heart's
Cusps and calluses

Weathers the existential
Fret over being or not being

Once in,
It elicits a thanking of Nature—God.

(1 September 2017, Regents Park)

To Tame a Horse

To tame it, you must first kill its soul;
The answering germ in its heart.
To arrest its ever-fervent spirit, you must
Keel it with deep bittersweetness.
To un-magic its spectral vision
You must blinker it with whispered love.
To feint it from coalescing with nature,
You must tether it to decadent luxury.
To keep it in love with your heavy scent,
You must cancel its sense of progeny.

(8 August 2024, 23:22 pm, Pokuase, Accra)

We the People

Here, we lie low, totally unoppressed, but
Fearful of our own voices. Broken dulcimers.
It's our past, you see; it ate our hearts and souls and
Perverted our judges and priests. Apostate thunder.
So question not this craven stare of ours.

Here the songbird scalds its own tongue
Not to sing truth, but a lilting howl to please devils.
It's the future, you see; it torments us with ghosts
Pummelled drunk by glib manifestos and deliria.
So question not our awkward place among nations.

Here, we govern ourselves unchecked, but
Weep when we reach our ecstasies. Shallow holes.
We take mud baths to exhaust our skin canker,
Rather than trounce our soul-eating canker.
For we are knee-deep in mire, fearing.

(26 September 2017, 10:40, London)

Promise of Feathers

Look, there's a woman praying in a firestorm;
She is singed, she has no feathers left on her back,
And she promises none – she wants water
Or shade, or a frog song to carry her dream in.

Beside her sits an emerald poultice of miracles,
Not for herself, but for those that need it more;
Those that have forded with their sickened hearts
The blackish rivers of want and maladroit polity,

Without a moon's shadow to guide their steps,
While hyenas lure them with children's voices,
From forlorn hilltops and precipices, and
Humble kudus snap at their heels for blood.

        She can't promise them feathers, but life.

For this firestorm is the fulfilment of a prophecy:
That man's passage will herald an end to nature,
For he knows not the in-between laws of
Balance and succour, but the joy of war.

(3 February 2021, London)

This Chief of Staff

Let it be known that I gave this thing a wide berth
Long before it formed any opinion of itself

Let it be known that others grew horny for it
For it elevated their self-hate to a bonfire

Let it be known that the thing tried riddling the pope
With the testimonies of an African-American martyr

Let it be known that the plagues and devastation are here
For this intransigent pharaoh contrives against love

Let it be known that the antichrist is finally come
And that it brings a deluge of heavy water in its wake.

Let it be known that a total eclipse has chimed in
To portend the cosmic bushelling to come

Let all this be known lest the thing gloss it with war.

(19 October, 2017, 1:35am, Regents Park, London)

24 February 1966

That Thursday came with flowers,
Garlands for the faux conquerors,
And a sick clap of foreign thunder.

The dogs stole behind bushes,
Dumb as broken bells, to watch a
Big history tumble into dead hands.

There was enough deadliness on the air
To haunt children for an eternity,
And music that fumed like quicklime.

Above all, there was the pantomime
Of feckless assholes and drug takers
Threshing out new myth to topple love.

Thus, Africa waned in its own sun.

(27 August, 2022, London)

These Scientists!

Unscrupulous people, scientists, each one of them:
They make TNT, H-Bomb, Cluster Bombs, Napalm,
Exocet, Anthrax, Luger, Uzi, M16, Kalashnikov, grenade,
Then blame religion for the cataclysm of war;

First they say the earth broke away from the moon,
Then change the story with the same sureness as the lie;
First they say the atom is the smallest indivisible thing,
Then split it for pogroms, but keep their old lie hanging;

The bastards, they murdered Hiroshima and Nagasaki—*they*!

They desecrate the graves of our ancestors,
To eliminate God from our genes, to usurp us;
Measure Tutankhamen's phallus and carry his corpse
Up and down the globe, like footsoldiers of a sick god;

Bunch of Mengeles, they say other beings are non-sentient,
To make us kill, eat, dissect and wear their skins with glee;
They GM our foods to addle the poor, then eat organic,
Because experimenting on fellow humans is their hobby;

The crooks even patent our DNA as personal property.

They breach the ozone layer with aviation fuel,
Rocket fuel, diesel, petrol, hell-fire, and factory clouds;
Make plastic, acid rain, radiation and heavy water, then
Blame cattle wind and poor agricos for global warming;

Without let, the liars traipse the decimated landscape
With uncanny sleight, scooing pious vespers like fairies,
Hogging the limelight with that ironic anthem of theirs:
"We have a short time, gov'ts must listen to the science!"

Thus, the vampires update themselves—to buy time.

(30 December 2021, London)

For Afro-Argentinians

Lineage

There is a jewelled, indigo vibration
Within your *own* aura that speaks
A faraway tongue; a most worshipful
Anagram for bright knowers only.

Sobriety stays far away from its orbit
Like the frayed edge of an old song,
Piping up, but fizzling into a sick echo—
Like the voice of false history.

    But does it despise sobriety so?

Nay, as a prophet may say, nay, but this is
The voice of untarnished royal blood,
Civilisation, valour, and love itself.
What is sobriety against such a voice?

(Sunday December 15, 2020, 12:04am, London)

On hearing of the imminent demise of JSVP[1]

A Great Sun Retires

When a great sun tires and turns its back on life,
Hope falls to its knees to remake prayer and song –
A paean rises through it's ancient sinews to play sun,
To shame the sallow moon from entering our orbit;

So that, we, acolytes of the sun, who know it better than
The myth makers, may carry its rays in us for posterity.

As the sun turns away, self-absolution becomes warfare,
A dark farce, a celebration of caveman misanthropy
That is too perverse to matter on the return of light,
And goodness suffers the acid pleasantries of guilt.

There is a love that dies to order (like a soldier's),
And there's a love that trounces death and its Anubis.

(8 July 2022, London)

1: Jill Silverman Van Coenegrachts

Parable of Tomorrow

It will happen, as before: the amnesiac's false tale
May sustain, till the bell tolls the almighty din,
Then the errant lore of avarice and iconoclasm
Will whimper, and stand aside for the translucent angel
To step out of her niche to take the reins of nature.

There will be no wars, for their sponsors will be gone;
There will be no duplicity, for there will be no politicians;
But there will be a grand destruction, a deep cleansing,
Then the oppressed shall walk their narrow paths again
And become the sages, kings, and gods of a new earth.

(1 August, 2023 to 19 April 2024, London and Accra)

Ladies and Others

Dear ladies and others,
Have you not seen the way
They toss you in dirt and acid
Like dubious metal, to assay you
For laughs and one-way rapture?

What are you waiting for?

(23 May 2021 to 21 April 2024, London & Accra)

For Palestine

Quietude

Don't sing like that, standing there
In those lederhosen and breeches—
Don't even think of it, you snake,
I am sleeping the sleep you killed,

When you buried our fathers alive.

Don't sing that hellish half song
Into this fist of love I have found
Between my two histories (don't you dare),
You stifler of Gods promise—coward.

Prick up your ears, *I* am singing now.

(7 January, 2020, 1:18 am, London)

For refugees

Bird Without Song

I don't land with crows or a song, proud me,
I don't bring locust clouds or rats or termites
To harass your land and God's sleep,
But a bottle of fireflies to light my way,
And a mother's prayer that I rise again.

(20 April 2024, Pokuase, Accra)

for Jesus the Christ

We May Never Know

We may never know who decided to kill him
On that barren hill with the crushing name, Golgotha—
It howls in us, whenever we remember him—;

Or if, the revelatory supper behind him, feet washed in turns,
And the enemy within outed poetically by his rapier mind,
He knew who awaited his coronation with purple irony;

> (but we know there were dogs on the street corners,
> whimpering and pre-mourning)

We may never know the colour of his imagining,
After parleying with the ghosts of his celestial ancestry,
Or if they'd decreed his ignominy as oblation for our sins;

While he anticipated the cowardice of his tiny army
In the face of his rendition unto the Caesar, though he knew
That the Pilate, a mere tweezer, was beneath him cosmically;

> (but we know a dreadfully bright sun rose early,
> to watch him dreadfully)

We may never know his state of mind, delirious or ecstatic,
As Pilate washed his trembling hands of his illicit lynching,
Amidst the fear-addled heaving and baying of the hordes;

Or if he craved the demise of the sun and its staunch mirages,
As he shouldered his stave alone towards the blood-soaked hill,
Where Anubis awaited him diffidently;

> (but we know there was a cicada on every leaf,
> eavesdropping for the moon)

We may never know if he saw crows or doves in his mind's eye
As he quizzed the eons, thorned and birched thin as he was,
Or if Gabriel whispered the prophecy in his ear;

While the red-eyed serpent peered from the back of his mind
Like a poacher's lookout on a grand, belittling manor,
Braced up for the weight of the forgiving smile;

> (but we know vagrants and beggars stood askance,
> to avoid the undertow)

We may never know what he saw in the faces baying at him;
Be it a bovine aspect, or the wretched sweetness of innocents
Pressed into buying imperious love with self-hate;

Or if he even saw the space craft circling Golgotha,
Awaiting his evacuation from flesh and anguish,
Or if, indeed, anguish blinded him to that kingly privilege;

> (but we know there were hawkers of food and stones,
> to test the Ascension)

We may never know if he felt the spear pierce his heart,
After seeking in vain the reprieve to alter the course of time,
Or if, indeed, it warmed his heart to the glory above;

Or if his mother's lingering smile freed his mind
For his globe-turning apotheosis; to embrace it
With the baffling grace of God, like John the Baptiser.

But we know he wept for us.

(23/3/2020, 03:05, Regents Park, London)

www.ingramcontent.com/pod-product-compliance
Lightning Source LLC
Chambersburg PA
CBHW042358280426
43661CB00096B/1150